VOICES · IN · POETRY

JOHN
KEATS

TEXT BY
PATRICIA KIRKPATRICK

ILLUSTRATIONS BY
ETIENNE DELESSERT

CREATIVE EDUCATION

This living hand, now warm and capable

Of earnest grasping, would, if it were cold

And in the icy silence of the tomb,

So haunt thy days and chill thy dreaming nights

That thou would wish thine own heart dry of blood,

So in my veins red life might stream again,

And thou be conscience-calm'd. See, here it is—

I hold it towards you.

From *Complete Poems: John Keats*

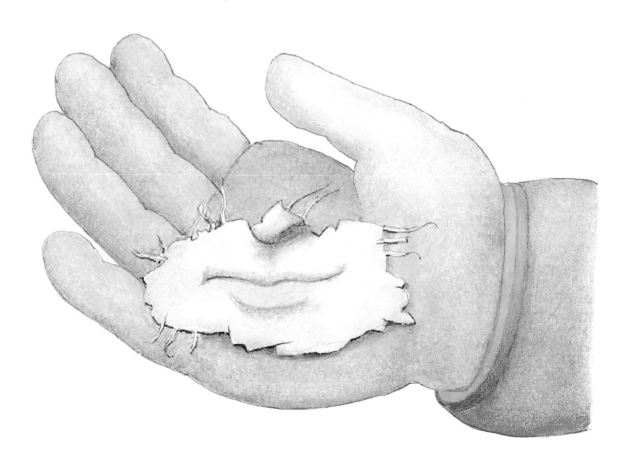

INTRODUCTION

*M*any of the qualities people associate with poetry today—beautiful sound, powerful language, images of the natural world, and the portrayal of strong feeling and emotional life—occur in the poetry of John Keats. Although his life and the years during which he wrote poetry were short, he wrote an astonishing variety and amount of poetry that people have continued to read, admire, and imitate for almost two centuries.

The poet Keats is often compared to is William Shakespeare, for like Shakespeare, Keats dramatically portrays the experience of being alive through musical phrasing, concrete imagery, and a sympathetic understanding of the subjects he describes. Keats admired Shakespeare greatly, and he often turned to Shakespeare's poetry and plays, as well as the historical legacy of English poetry, once writing, "I think I shall be among the English poets after my death." Indeed, Keats's gifts as a poet have placed him among the world's greatest poets, but in the words of a noted English scholar, "Keats was not only a poet of genius but a noble, affectionate, and suffering human being."

THE STABLE

John Keats was born in London, England, in 1795, the oldest child of Thomas and Frances Keats. His father worked as a head hostler, or stableman, in a livery stable that supplied horses for carriages traveling from London to northern England. John's mother, the daughter of the stable's owner, was a lively and passionate woman especially devoted to her son John. John soon had three brothers: George, born in 1797; Thomas, born in 1799; and Edward, who died in infancy in 1801. A sister, Frances Mary, known as Fanny, was born in 1803.

The family lived in an apartment over the stable, and perhaps being so close to the stable's animals and physical sensations influenced John's love of the natural world. A Keats biographer later wrote, "The stableyard was the scene of constant comings and goings, of shouts and neighs and clattering hoofs, of jingling harness and gleaming horseflesh, of strong smells and swift movement that would fill a small boy with delight."

The Keats family was prosperous, and John and his brother George were sent to a good school in the nearby village of Enfield. But John showed little interest in or promise at school; in fact, his fellow schoolmates recalled his fierce courage as a fighter and assumed that he would make a name for himself in the military. John enjoyed practical jokes, excelled at sports, and, as one acquaintance noted, "would fight anyone, morning, noon, or night."

Tragedy, however, soon changed the course of John's life. When he was nine, his father was killed in a riding accident. His mother remarried, and the Keats children went to live with their grandparents. But more tragedy followed. When John's mother contracted tuberculosis, she moved in with her parents and children, and John himself nursed her until her death in 1810.

His parents' deaths transformed John from a lively, high-spirited boy to one of serious purpose. He had discovered the school library and now began spending all of his free time reading both contemporary and ancient writers, including the fantastic romances of Edmund Spenser, the poems and plays of William Shakespeare, and plenty of Greek mythology. In 1811, eager to find a purpose and make his mark, he left home and school to begin an apprenticeship as a doctor.

After their grandmother died in 1814, the remaining Keats children were separated by Richard Abbey, the guardian she had chosen for them. George went to work in Abbey's London business; Tom and Fanny moved into the Abbey household. Keats later told a friend, "I have never known any unalloyed happiness for many days together: the death or sickness of some one has always spoilt my hours."

I HAD A DOVE, AND THE SWEET DOVE DIED

I had a dove, and the sweet dove died,

    And I have thought it died of grieving;

O what could it grieve for? Its feet were tied

    With a silken thread of my own hand's weaving:

        Sweet little red feet! why would you die?

        Why would you leave me, sweet bird, why?

You liv'd alone on the forest tree,

Why, pretty thing, could you not live with me?

    I kiss'd you oft, and gave you white pease;

    Why not live sweetly as in the green trees?

        From *Complete Poems: John Keats*

APPRENTICE

When Keats left school in 1811, he became apprenticed to an apothecary-surgeon, with whom he lived in a neighboring village. At first, he was still able to visit his grandparents and siblings, and in the evenings, he continued to walk to his old school to discuss literature and poems with a friend, Charles Cowden Clarke. Clarke later wrote of Keats's pleasure in the sounds and imagery of poetry, remembering how when he and Keats read a long poem aloud together, Keats went through it "like a young horse turned into a spring meadow."

At age 19, after four years as an apprentice, Keats moved to London to become a medical student at Guy's Hospital. While attending lectures and working exhausting hours in the hospital wards, Keats also was apprenticing himself to poetry, continuing to read Shakespeare and John Milton, as well as other poets of the day, such as Percy Bysshe Shelley and William Wordsworth. Eventually, Keats began to write poetry himself and to meet other

An early 19th-century London bookshop

writers. In London, he also visited his brothers George, who remained his closest friend, and Tom, who had moved to the city and begun to show the first signs of tuberculosis. Keats wrote regularly to his sister, feeling a father's tenderness for the dutiful girl who remained behind in the "stale respectability" of the Abbey home.

In 1816, Keats published his first poem, "O Solitude." That same year, he also published "On First Looking into Chapman's Homer," considered by many to be the first "great" poem Keats wrote. In some ways, that poem is about Keats's apprenticeship as a poet, for it describes a speaker's excitement when he reads a new translation of the ancient Greek story the *Odyssey*, comparing that excitement to an explorer's when he first sees the Pacific Ocean. The poem carries some of the excitement of pure discovery itself. Although Keats was devoted to his patients and diligent in his studies, by 1817, his passion for literature was greater than his feeling for medicine. That year, he published his first book, *Poems*, and gave up his pursuit of a medical career altogether.

Much have I travell'd in the realms of gold,

   And many goodly states and kingdoms seen;

   Round many western islands have I been

Which bards in fealty to Apollo hold.

Oft of one wide expanse had I been told

   That deep-brow'd Homer ruled as his demesne;

   Yet did I never breathe its pure serene

Till I heard Chapman speak out loud and bold:

Then felt I like some watcher of the skies

   When a new planet swims into his ken;

Or like stout Cortez when with eagle eyes

   He star'd at the Pacific—and all his men

Look'd at each other with a wild surmise—

   Silent, upon a peak in Darien.

From *Poems*

Percy Bysshe Shelley (1792–1822)

Leigh Hunt (1784–1859)

Samuel Coleridge (1772–1834)

William Wordsworth (1770–1850)

John Keats (1795–1821)

*K*eats had read and been influenced by many of the great English poetic forms, especially the dramas of Shakespeare and the long epic, or narrative, poems of John Milton. In 1817, he began writing his own long poem, "Endymion," a work of about 4,000 lines, in which Keats explored the struggle between accepting the world as it is and yearning for an ideal world.

But Keats was also interested in a new direction in poetry, something he called "thinking into the heart." In the early part of the 19th century, Keats, as well as other poets such as William Wordsworth, Samuel Coleridge, and Percy Bysshe Shelley, began to turn away from the idea of poetry as a means of writing about ideal situations and heroic adventures and instead began to write about the real world with concrete details of its beauty and suffering. These poets, who later came to be known as the "Romantics," admired immediacy and naturalness in writing, which they believed brought readers "closer to the actual poet and to actual experience."

Once Keats set his sights on "the horizon of poetry," he became associated with the new poetry of the Romantics. In London, he made the acquaintance of writer and leading political journalist of the day Leigh Hunt, and through Hunt met many writers, editors, artists, and philosophers. He frequented the city's bookshops and galleries and attended plays, lectures, and evening parties lively with wine and conversation. When Hunt published an article entitled "Young Poets," he introduced the work of Percy Bysshe Shelley, "a striking and original thinker"; John Reynolds, a friend of Keats; and John Keats, whom Hunt considered the most promising of the three. Although Keats's first book of poetry received scarce public attention, he sensed that he stood on the threshold that linked the great poetry of the English past—Chaucer, Milton, and Shakespeare—with the new "poetry of the wide world."

O thou whose face hath felt the winter's wind,

Whose eye has seen the snow clouds hung in mist,

And the black-elm tops 'mong the freezing stars,

To thee the spring will be a harvest-time.

O thou whose only book has been the light

Of supreme darkness which thou feddest on

Night after night, when Phœbus was away,

To thee the spring shall be a tripple morn.

O fret not after knowledge—I have none,

And yet my song comes native with the warmth;

O fret not after knowledge—I have none,

And yet the evening listens. He who saddens

At thought of idleness cannot be idle,

And he's awake who thinks himself asleep.

From *Complete Poems: John Keats*

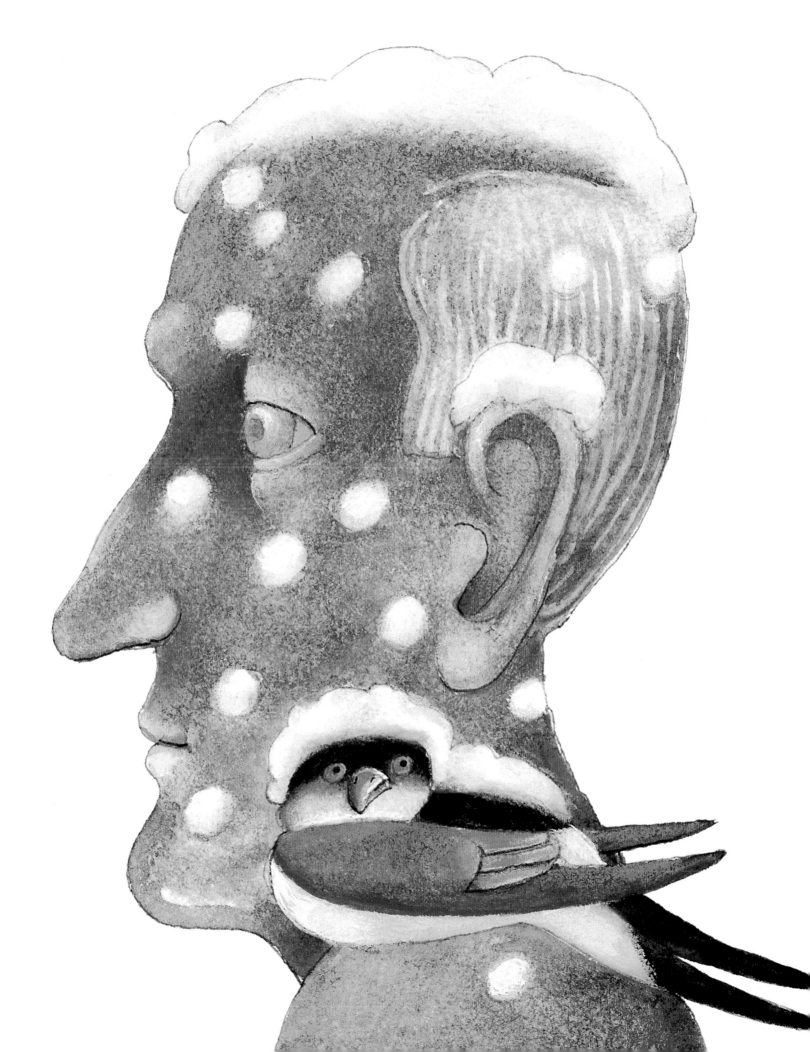

LETTERS

Some of Keats's poems, as well as his ideas about poetry and the life of a poet, appear in the many letters he wrote to his family and friends. Keats's letters are important not only because they are filled with good humor, descriptions, observations, feelings, and details about his daily life, but because they reflect Keats's personality and his development as a poet in what was to be a tragically short career.

Keats wrote his letters spontaneously, often during periods when he was not writing poetry. In fact, he had begun to see a pattern in his creative process: a period of great energy and output would often be followed by inactivity—"idleness," as he called it. He came to trust such idleness. As he wrote to a friend, "Let us not therefore go hurrying about and collect-

ing honey, beelike buzzing here and there impatiently from a knowledge of what is to be arrived at but let us open our leaves like a flower and be passive and receptive. . . . I was lead into these thoughts, my dear Reynolds, by the beauty of the morning operating on a sense of Idleness—I had no Idea but of the Morning and the Thrush said I was right."

Keats was stimulated by life in London, but he also grew restless in the city. So, in 1817, he moved with his brothers to Hampstead Heath, the open fields on the north edge of London. There he loved to walk for hours, lie in the grass to read, and listen to the wind and birds. His richly worded letters led one Keats biographer to note, "Evidently his boyhood absorption in the hidden life of nature had only been intensified by his training in close observation as a medical student."

An 1828 painting of Hampstead Heath

TO GEORGE AND GEORGIANA KEATS

[March 19, 1819]

*Y*esterday I got a black eye—the first time I took a Cr[icket] bat—Brown who is always

one's friend in a disaster [app]lied a lee[ch to] the eyelid, and there is no infla[mm]ation

this morning though the ball hit me dir[ectl]y on the sight—'t was a white ball—I am glad

it was not a clout—This is the second black eye I have had since leaving school—during all

my [scho]ol days I never had one at all—we must e[a]t a peck before we die. . . . I go among

the Fields and catch a glimpse of a stoat or a fieldmouse peeping out of the withered grass—

the creature hath a purpose and its eyes are bright with it—I go amongst the buildings of a

city and I see a Man hurrying along—to what? The Creature has a purpose and his eyes are

bright with it. But then as Wordsworth says, "we have all one human heart"—there is an

ellectric fire in human nature tending to purify—so that among these human creature[s]

there is continu[a]lly some birth of new heroism. . . .

From *Life, Letters, and Literary Remains of John Keats*

SPARROW

One of Keats's most important insights, the idea of "negative capability," continues to influence poets and writers nearly 200 years later. It first appeared in a letter written to his brothers in 1817: "Several things dovetailed in my mind, & at once it struck me, what qualities went to form a Man of Achievement especially in Literature & which Shakespeare posessed [sic] so enormously—I mean Negative Capability, that is when man is capable of being in uncertainties, Mysteries, doubts, without any irritable reaching after fact & reason."

According to Keats, negative capability means that not only do poets need to be able to live with uncertainties, mysteries, and doubt when they are trying to write, but they must also put their own identities aside to best observe other creatures, imagine their inner lives, and consider the possibility of other ideas. The most famous example of negative capability in Keats's own work comes at the end of a letter he wrote to his friend Benjamin Bailey in 1817. Keats's comment "if a Sparrow come before my Window I take part in its existince [sic] and pick about the Gravel" often has been paraphrased to mean "If you want to write about a sparrow, you must become a sparrow."

The rolling green countryside of early 19th-century Scotland

In 1818, Keats's brother George married and moved to America, and the care of their brother Tom, whose tuberculosis had advanced seriously, fell exclusively to Keats. Keats kept up a brave front, for he was hopeful that Tom would recover. When Tom's health improved in the summer, Keats was able to leave London for a walking tour of Scotland with a friend. Many of the places they visited were mentioned in a novel by Sir Walter Scott. As Keats walked along the craggy rocks overgrown with bramble and wild roses, he felt he was visiting the very spot where one of the novel's characters, Meg Merrilies, had "boiled her kettle." Keats described the countryside in a letter to Tom, praising the neat cottages "squat among trees and fern," and the fields and bushes of broom "on levels, slopes, and heights." He also wrote that he would rather be a wild deer than a girl who had to obey the Scottish church, or "Kirk," and rather be a wild hog than a poor person who had to pay dues to the church elders.

In the same letter, Keats included a "song" telling his version of the Meg Merrilies story. Keats's song "Old Meg" is written as a ballad. A ballad is a poem or song that tells a story; it is written in stanzas of four lines, or quatrains, and the second and fourth line of a quatrain usually rhyme. Although Keats's ballad depicts Old Meg having a rather rough life, it also includes images of what Keats admired in the Scottish countryside.

Unfortunately, when Keats returned to London that fall, he found that his brother's health had greatly deteriorated. Keats nursed Tom through the fall, and on December 1, 1818, Tom Keats died.

OLD MEG SHE WAS A GIPSEY

Old Meg she was a gipsey,
    And liv'd upon the moors;
Her bed it was the brown heath turf,
    And her house was out of doors.

Her apples were swart blackberries,
    Her currants pods o' broom,
Her wine was dew o' the wild white rose,
    Her book a churchyard tomb.

Her brothers were the craggy hills,
    Her sisters larchen trees—
Alone with her great family
    She liv'd as she did please.

No breakfast had she many a morn,
    No dinner many a noon,
And 'stead of supper she would stare
    Full hard against the moon.

But every morn of woodbine fresh
    She made her garlanding,
And every night the dark glen yew
    She wove and she would sing.

And with her fingers old and brown
    She plaited mats o' rushes,
And gave them to the cottagers
    She met among the bushes.

Old Meg was brave as Margaret Queen
    And tall as Amazon:
An old red blanket cloak she wore;
    A chip hat had she on.
God rest her aged bones somewhere—
    She died full long agone!

From *Complete Poems: John Keats*

B R I G H T   S T A R

While in London nursing his brother, Keats met 18-year-old Fanny Brawne and experienced the "bright star" of romantic love for the first time. Keats was 23. He had enjoyed the company and friendship of many men and women, but he had never fallen deeply in love. Now, often he could think of nothing but Fanny. Keats described her as "beautiful and elegant, graceful, silly, fashionable and strange." By Christmas of that year, he and Fanny had come to an "understanding" about their feelings for each other.

Yet Keats remained torn between his love for Fanny, his tremendous ambition as a poet, and the uncertainty of his own health and finances. In the summer of 1819, Keats left Hampstead for a season of solitude on the English Isle of Wight. There, he wrote Fanny what has become one of his most famous sonnets, "Bright star, would I were stedfast as thou art." A sonnet is a traditional poetic form that was popular in the 14th through 17th centuries; Keats helped make the sonnet popular again in the 19th century and beyond. The word "sonnet," from the Italian *sonetto*, means "little song." It is a lyric poem, 14 lines long, usually rhymed, and historically focused on the subject of love.

In the poem "Bright Star," the speaker wishes to be as unchanging as his beloved, not to be alone in the night like a hermit or "eremite," but to be beside her, feeling her breathe, restless and happy because she is near. Scholars believe Keats often felt unsteady in his relationship with Fanny because he was separated from her, or because he was ill, felt jealous, or remained too poor to get married.

Bright star, would I were stedfast as thou art—

    Not in lone splendor hung aloft the night,

And watching, with eternal lids apart,

    Like nature's patient, sleepless eremite,

The moving waters at their priestlike task

    Of pure ablution round earth's human shores,

Or gazing on the new soft-fallen mask

Of snow upon the mountains and the moors;

No—yet still stedfast, still unchangeable,

    Pillow'd upon my fair love's ripening breast,

To feel for ever its soft swell and fall,

    Awake for ever in a sweet unrest,

Still, still to hear her tender-taken breath,

And so live ever—or else swoon to death.

From The Poetical Works of John Keats

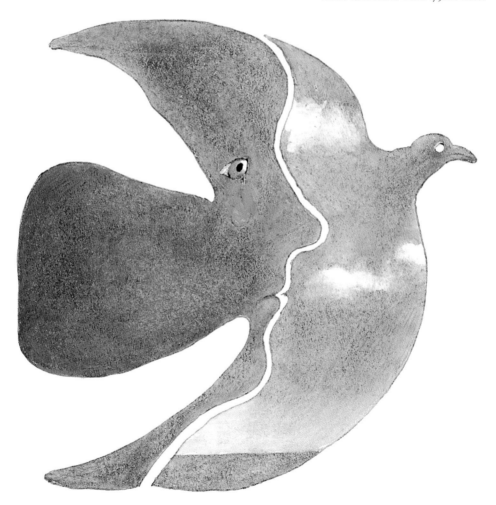

DEATH WARRANT

*B*y 1819, Keats was sharing a house in Hampstead with a friend; Fanny Brawne and her family lived next door. He was suffering from a sore throat and a shortage of money. Yet that same year he was also working at the height of his powers as a poet and writing the most important poetry of his life. During an astonishing outpouring of creative energy that began in the spring and lasted for five months, Keats completed the long romance "The Eve of St. Agnes" and wrote "The Belle Dame Sans Merci." He also wrote all of his major odes except "To Autumn," which he wrote in September. But something was wrong. His sore throat would not go away, and he was exhausted and demoralized. Perhaps in his heart he knew that, like his mother and brother, he too had tuberculosis.

One night in early 1820, Keats returned home with a severe chill and was urged to go to bed. As he got into his bed, he coughed slightly and saw a spot of blood on the sheet. "Bring me a candle," Keats asked his friend, and then calmly examined the blood he knew he had coughed from his lungs, a sure sign of tuberculosis. "I know the colour of that blood," he stated. "It is arterial blood—I cannot be deceived in that colour; that drop is my death warrant. I must die."

He had spoken the truth. Good and bad days followed. In July, a volume of his poems, *Lamia, Isabella, The Eve of St. Agnes, and Other Poems*, was published. Fanny Brawne nursed him through the summer, and Keats watched her walk past his window to the heath. He wrote his siblings letters from his bed, and Fanny also corresponded with Keats's sister to keep her informed of his illness.

Keats's Hampstead home, photographed in 1931

When I have fears that I may cease to be

Before my pen has glean'd my teeming brain,

Before high piled books, in charactry,

Hold like rich garners the full ripen'd grain;

When I behold, upon the night's starr'd face,

Huge cloudy symbols of a high romance,

And think that I may never live to trace

Their shadows, with the magic hand of chance;

And when I feel, fair creature of an hour,

That I shall never look upon thee more,

Never have relish in the fairy power

Of unreflecting love;—then on the shore

Of the wide world I stand alone, and think

Till love and fame to nothingness do sink.

From *The Poetical Works of John Keats*

NIGHTINGALE

One of the most famous poems Keats wrote is "Ode to a Nightingale." An ode is a poem of praise and celebration that can take many forms; this ode is written in 8 stanzas of 10 lines each. In it, Keats praises the nightingale, which the speaker of his poem cannot see but senses "In some melodious plot / Of beechen green, and shadows numberless." In the second section of the poem, the speaker wonders if he "might drink, and leave the world unseen" and with the nightingale "fade away into the forest dim." These are some of the concrete details the Romantic poets were famous for: "The grass, the thicket, and the fruit-tree wild; / White hawthorn, and the pastoral eglantine; / Fast fading violets cover'd up in leaves." Such details make the nightingale seem very real, and yet it is very much more than a bird, of course; it is an urgent presence pouring forth a mysterious song heard in both ancient times and on this passing night.

"Ode to a Nightingale" is a rich and complex poem, full of music and puzzles that may not be immediately clear to readers on a first or second reading. Reading the poem aloud and listening to its music as the speaker of the poem listens to the nightingale can help readers feel the beauty Keats describes and wonder at the questions he explores.

A portrait of Keats by Joseph Severn

1

My heart aches, and a drowsy numbness pains
    My sense, as though of hemlock I had drunk,
Or emptied some dull opiate to the drains
    One minute past, and Lethe-wards had sunk:
'Tis not through envy of thy happy lot,
    But being too happy in thine happiness,—
        That thou, light-winged Dryad of the trees,
            In some melodious plot
    Of beechen green, and shadows numberless,
        Singest of summer in full-throated ease.

2

O, for a draught of vintage! that hath been
    Cool'd a long age in the deep-delved earth,
Tasting of Flora and the country green,
    Dance, and Provençal song, and sunburnt mirth!
O for a beaker full of the warm South,
    Full of the true, the blushful Hippocrene,
        With beaded bubbles winking at the brim,
            And purple-stained mouth;
    That I might drink, and leave the world unseen,
        And with thee fade away into the forest dim:

3

Fade far away, dissolve, and quite forget
    What thou among the leaves hast never known,
The weariness, the fever, and the fret
    Here, where men sit and hear each other groan;
Where palsy shakes a few, sad, last gray hairs,
    Where youth grows pale, and spectre-thin, and dies;
        Where but to think is to be full of sorrow
            And leaden-eyed despairs,
Where Beauty cannot keep her lustrous eyes,
    Or new Love pine at them beyond to-morrow.

4

Away! away! for I will fly to thee,

    Not charioted by Bacchus and his pards,

But on the viewless wings of Poesy,

    Though the dull brain perplexes and retards:

Already with thee! tender is the night,

    And haply the Queen-Moon is on her throne,

        Cluster'd around by all her starry Fays;

        But here there is no light,

    Save what from heaven is with the breezes blown

        Through verdurous glooms and winding mossy ways.

5

I cannot see what flowers are at my feet,

    Nor what soft incense hangs upon the boughs,

But, in embalmed darkness, guess each sweet

    Wherewith the seasonable month endows

The grass, the thicket, and the fruit-tree wild;

    White hawthorn, and the pastoral eglantine;

        Fast fading violets cover'd up in leaves;

        And mid-May's eldest child,

The coming musk-rose, full of dewy wine,

        The murmurous haunt of flies on summer eves.

6

Darkling I listen; and, for many a time

    I have been half in love with easeful Death,

Call'd him soft names in many a mused rhyme,

    To take into the air my quiet breath;

Now more than ever seems it rich to die,

To cease upon the midnight with no pain,

While thou art pouring forth thy soul abroad

In such an ecstasy!

Still wouldst thou sing, and I have ears in vain—

To thy high requiem become a sod.

7

Thou wast not born for death, immortal Bird!

No hungry generations tread thee down;

The voice I hear this passing night was heard

In ancient days by emperor and clown:

Perhaps the self-same song that found a path

Through the sad heart of Ruth, when, sick for home,

She stood in tears amid the alien corn;

The same that oft-times hath

Charm'd magic casements, opening on the foam

Of perilous seas, in faery lands forlorn.

8

Forlorn! the very word is like a bell

To toll me back from thee to my sole self!

Adieu! the fancy cannot cheat so well

As she is fam'd to do, deceiving elf.

Adieu! adieu! thy plaintive anthem fades

Past the near meadows, over the still stream,

Up the hill-side; and now 'tis buried deep

In the next valley-glades:

Was it a vision, or a waking dream?

Fled is that music:—Do I wake or sleep?

From *Lamia, Isabella, The Eve of St. Agnes, and Other Poems*

An artistic rendering of Rome, Italy, in Keats's time

"God alone knows whether I am destined to taste of happiness with you," Keats had written to Fanny Brawne when he knew he had tuberculosis. "At all events I myself know this much, that I consider it no mean happiness to have loved you thus far—if it is to be no farther I shall not be unthankful."

Keats did not get better. In August 1820, his doctors convinced him that he could not survive another English winter. With his friend, a young painter named Joseph Severn, Keats sailed to sunny Italy, settling in Rome.

The last three months of Keats's life were painful, not only because he suffered physically, but because he knew what he had lost—his beloved Fanny, his dear friends, and the valuable time needed to write the poetry he was capable of writing. When all hope was lost for his recovery, he bitterly regretted that he would die far away from those he loved. Yet Joseph Severn reported that Keats died peacefully, saying at the end, "Don't be frightened—be firm, and thank God it has come." On February 23, 1821, at age 25, John Keats was dead.

TO AUTUMN

1

*S*eason of mists and mellow fruitfulness,

    Close bosom-friend of the maturing sun;

Conspiring with him how to load and bless

    With fruit the vines that round the thatch-eves run;

To bend with apples the moss'd cottage-trees,

    And fill all fruit with ripeness to the core;

        To swell the gourd, and plump the hazel shells

    With a sweet kernel; to set budding more,

And still more, later flowers for the bees,

Until they think warm days will never cease,

        For summer has o'er-brimm'd their clammy cells.

2

Who hath not seen thee oft amid thy store?

Sometimes whoever seeks abroad may find

Thee sitting careless on a granary floor,

Thy hair soft-lifted by the winnowing wind;

Or on a half-reap'd furrow sound asleep,

Drows'd with the fume of poppies, while thy hook

Spares the next swath and all its twined flowers:

And sometimes like a gleaner thou dost keep

Steady thy laden head across a brook;

Or by a cyder-press, with patient look,

Thou watchest the last oozings hours by hours.

3

Where are the songs of spring? Ay, where are they?

Think not of them, thou hast thy music too,—

While barred clouds bloom the soft-dying day,

And touch the stubble-plains with rosy hue;

Then in a wailful choir the small gnats mourn

Among the river sallows, borne aloft

Or sinking as the light wind lives or dies;

And full-grown lambs loud bleat from hilly bourn;

Hedge-crickets sing; and now with treble soft

The red-breast whistles from a garden-croft;

And gathering swallows twitter in the skies.

From *Lamia, Isabella, The Eve of St. Agnes, and Other Poems*

ENDYMION: BOOK I. ❀ ❀ ❀ ❀ ❀

A THING OF BEAUTY
IS A JOY FOR EVER:
ITS LOVELINESS IN
CREAS...
NEVER...
NOTH...
...BUT...
KEEP A BOWER QU...
AND A SLEEP FULL...
DREAMS, & HEALT...
BREATHING 🍃 T...
ON EVERY MORRO...
WREATHING A FLO...
TO BIND US TO TH...
SPITE OF DESPON...
THE INHUMAN DEA...
BLE NATURES, OF T...
DAYS, OF ALL THE U...
AND O'ER-DARKE...
MADE FOR OUR SEA...
IN SPITE OF ALL, S...
OF BEAUTY MOVES...
PALL FROM OUR DA...
🍃 SUCH THE SUN, THE MOON,
TREES OLD & YOUNG, SPROUT,
ING A SHADY BOON FOR SIMPLE
SHEEP; & SUCH ARE DAFFODILS

An 1894 publication of Keats's "Endymion"

EPITAPH

Keats had asked that the epitaph on his gravestone read simply, "Here lies one whose name was writ in water," and so his stone reads on a grassy slope in the Protestant cemetery in Rome.

But the name of John Keats has not disappeared in water. Keats's reputation grew steadily after his death, and today he is regarded as one of the finest poets who has written in the English language. His ambition, accomplishments, and mastery of form were great, but his gift to readers is in many ways simple: his poems remind readers of what it is to be a human being, to love, and laugh, and grieve, and wonder, and hope; to praise the world that can be seen and heard, and to approach the world beyond it which can only be sensed. "Heard melodies are sweet, but those unheard / Are sweeter; therefore, ye soft pipes, play on" Keats wrote in his famous poem "Ode on a Grecian Urn."

For John Keats, the human imagination was the bridge between the known and unknown worlds and "what the imagination seizes as Beauty must be truth." "Ode on a Grecian Urn" ends with perhaps Keats's most famous lines: "'Beauty is truth, truth beauty,'—that is all / Ye know on earth, and all ye need to know."

K-eats! if thy cherished name be "writ in water"
E-ach drop has fallen from some mourner's cheek;
A-sacred tribute; such as heroes seek,
T-hough oft in vain—for dazzling deeds of slaughter
S-leep on! Not honoured less for Epitaph so meek!

A John Keats memorial plaque in Rome

ON THE GRASSHOPPER AND CRICKET

The poetry of earth is never dead:

　　When all the birds are faint with the hot sun,

　　And hide in cooling trees, a voice will run

From hedge to hedge about the new-mown mead;

That is the Grasshopper's—he takes the lead

　　In summer luxury,—he has never done

　　With his delights; for when tired out with fun

He rests at ease beneath some pleasant weed.

The poetry of earth is ceasing never:

　　On a lone winter evening, when the frost

　　　　Has wrought a silence, from the stove there shrills

The Cricket's song, in warmth increasing ever,

　　And seems to one in drowsiness half lost,

　　　　The Grasshopper's among some grassy hills.

From *Poems*

ACKNOWLEDGMENTS

PHOTO CREDITS

Photographs by Corbis (Archivo Iconografico, S.A., Bettmann, Edimédia, Fine Art Photographic Library, Historical Picture Archive, Hulton-Deutsch Collection, Bill Ross, Stapleton Collection), Getty Images (Hulton Archive), The Granger Collection, New York

ILLUSTRATION CREDITS

Illustrations on cover and pages 1, 3, 5, 10–11, 14, 19, 22, 26, 29, 32, 35, 36–37, 40, 41, and 44–45 by Etienne Delessert.
Copyright © 2006 Etienne Delessert.

SELECTED WORKS BY JOHN KEATS

POETRY

Poems, 1817
Endymion: A Poetic Romance, 1818
Lamia, Isabella, The Eve of St. Agnes, and Other Poems, 1820

NOTABLE POSTHUMOUS WORKS

Life, Letters, and Literary Remains of John Keats, 1848
The Poetical Works of John Keats, 1884
The Letters of John Keats, 1814–1821, 1958
Complete Poems: John Keats, 1991

Published by Creative Education
123 South Broad Street, Mankato, Minnesota 56001
Creative Education is an imprint of The Creative Company
Copyright © 2006 Creative Education
Illustrations copyright © 2006 Etienne Delessert

Art direction by Rita Marshall; Design by Stephanie Blumenthal
Production design by Melinda Belter
Printed in Italy.
Library of Congress Cataloging-in-Publication Data
Kirkpatrick, Patricia.
John Keats / by Patricia Kirkpatrick.
p. cm. — (Voices in poetry)
Includes index.
ISBN 1-58341-345-6
1. Keats, John, 1795-1821—Juvenile literature. 2. Poets, English,
19th century—Biography—Juvenile literature. I. Title. II. Voices in
poetry (Mankato, Minn.)
PR4836.K57 2005   821'.7—dc22   2004059341 [B]

First Edition
9 8 7 6 5 4 3 2 1